Choose  ..nge:

It's your life

Easy Steps to Live the Life of Your Dreams

Jacqui Penn

Copyright © 2017 Jacqui Penn

Contents

Introduction 5

How to use this book 10

1 - No Excuses 11

2 - Tell the Truth 17

3 - Let it go 22

4 - Admit you're wrong 27

5 - Forgive 30

6 - Positive thinking 34

Part 2 - The new you! 39

7 - Find your happiness 41

8 - Be who you want to be 47

9 - Small steps 51

10 - Blow away the cobwebs 56

11 - Wake up earlier 60

12 - Talk yourself into something good 64

13 - Understand your triggers 70

14 - Choose your friends 74

Author note 78

15 - Feeling Good 81

16 - Make a list 85

17 - How are you doing? 89

18 - Take a moment to choose 93

19 - Open your world 97

20 - Just do it anyway! 101

21 - Step out of your comfort zone 104

22 - Walk tall 108

23 - Your glass is always full 112

24 - Life isn't a competition 115

25 - Are you proud of yourself? 119

Checklist and Journal Offer 123

Other Books by Jacqui Penn 124

Links mentioned 125

Acknowledgements 126

About Jacqui 127

Introduction

We all need something to feel good about, and the good thing right now is that you are reading this book. The next good thing is that you've realised that maybe things in your life are not as good as they could be, and you want to do something about that. You're already streets ahead. There are many times in our lives when things are not going so well. These times define who we are, and with a positive approach, they make us stronger. Always remember there is no light without dark, and no good without bad. How would we define light without having dark?

Our thoughts, whether negative or positive, stem from our inner self, our mind. It could be said that our actions are a direct consequence of our subconscious programming, and that those thoughts impede our need for peace of mind and impact on our mood and feelings.

Have you ever tried to stop having thoughts for only a minute? How many times have you wanted to stop thinking about something and be free from a concern that's playing on your mind? So do we have to change our thoughts to achieve peace? To a certain extent yes, but we also have to accept that inner peace can't be bought or found, it can't be achieved by a continuous struggle to find it.

Peace is already within us; we were born into this world with everything we needed. So what happened to our peace of mind? We began to struggle and allowed our thoughts to provoke stress and infringe on our happiness. We allowed negativity to creep in and change us. It could be said that our experience, passed on through generations, has taught us to allow and accept negativity.

Many people go through their life not realising that they have the power to choose how they feel and create their own identity. Two people can be faced with the same situation, but choose to deal with it differently. How you choose to confront situations will determine your mind set. A positive attitude, and a willingness to let go will move you forward into a happier mind set. If you let past, negative thoughts rule, then you are not using the power you have. If you decide to find some positive thoughts, then you are on the way to finding inner peace.

Do you truly want to change anything in your life or do you believe *it's just the way I am?* When you bought this

7

book you took the first step towards changing. I can't make the changes for you, but you can. You have the power and the choice to unleash the person you want to be, and I will help you every step of the way.

Short easily digestible chapters and easy to implement exercises will set you on the road to a more evolved, happier you, if that's what you want. Did you know that anything is possible if you want it enough and have the willpower to keep moving forward? Thomas Edison, Abraham Lincoln, J K Rowling, Barak Obama, and Colonel Sanders, to name a few, have given us wonderful examples of striving to achieve a goal. If you're determined to choose a new direction, then you're in the right place.

There will be doubters amongst you, and those are the people who, for the foreseeable future, will be living the life they have now. Don't join them. Walk in the opposite direction and believe in yourself. Choose a new path right now.

Don't think you have to master everything at once—just make a small step in the right direction. Make today better than yesterday.

I've found inner peace, and with my Choose to Change plan, so can you. Don't worry about the destination, come with me and enjoy the journey to the fulfilled, peaceful, happy life you want and deserve.

If you are going to flick through the pages of this book and not implement any of the content, nothing will change. Make a promise to yourself that you are going to implement at least one thing every day to work towards your goals. Make that promise and keep to your word.

How to use this book

I would suggest you read one chapter and try to dive straight into the ideas. *"Don't put off until tomorrow what you can do today"* Benjamin Franklin ... *"A year from now you may wish you had started today"* Karen Lamb ... *"The best way to get something done, is to begin"* Author unknown ... *"and begin you must"* (That last one was me!) Seriously, the sooner you start, the sooner little changes will begin to make a difference.

Download a handy checklist using the link on page 123. It'll help keep track, and act as a great reminder of what you'd like to take a look at again.

Keep a note of chapters that you really like and keep your journal going. If you haven´t downloaded your free journal yet, get it now by following the link at the end of the book on page 123.

Life balance is the key—let's get started with the first step of the journey.

1 - No Excuses

If you want a different life, you need an open mind that enables you to do different things. Change can't happen if you're not prepared to change. The second you decide to change; you have pressed that all important start button—this is where you begin to decide your future.

Anyone can change, but you really have to believe that *you* can. Some people are too ready to make excuses and carry on feeling unsatisfied. We can all come up with reasons for keeping things the way they are. *I couldn't do that. It's just not me. This is the way I've always been. I'm too set in my ways to change now. I can't help the way I feel.* If you make excuses, you're not serious about wanting a happier life.

It takes strength to change. You have to be determined and stick with your plan. How do artists get good at what they do? They practice, they get it wrong, and they try again. No one was born being able to draw, play an instrument or write a book; practice and more practice is the only way to improve and accomplish your dream.

So this is where we begin. Maybe you've let bad habits and negative thoughts take over and infringe on your happiness. Nothing in life is set in stone. Let's try a quick exercise - you'll need a pen and paper.

Think of one thing in your life that you'd like to change to make you feel happier. Write it down. Now think of one thing you could do to change the situation.

Did you come up with an excuse before you wrote how to change the situation? Most people will have done just that. If you didn't come up with an excuse, can you implement the change? If not, maybe take a step back and think of five smaller steps to aim you in the right direction. Sometimes the things we want to change are not possible, but it is possible to change the way we think.

"Using the power of decision gives you the capacity to get past any excuse to change any and every part of your life in an instant."

Anthony Robbins

Think about what you wanted to change. Was it material? Maybe the car, the job, the house, the relationship you want is out of reach at the moment, but as I already said, nothing is set in stone, and who knows what lies ahead? Inner peace will come if you appreciate what you already have instead of chasing something better. That is not to say it isn't good to have a dream, but just don't go chasing it or you will lose your happiness on the way. Every day is a blessing and you need to live for today; not for what happened yesterday or what might happen tomorrow. Buddha sums this up, *"The secret of health for both mind and body is not to mourn for the past, worry about the future, or anticipate troubles, but to live in the present moment wisely and earnestly."*

In the previous exercise, if you wrote about something on your mind you'd like to change, is someone or something really stopping you, or are you making an excuse? Is there one tiny thing you could change to make it better for yourself?

Do this exercise without making any excuses. With the thing you'd like to change on your mind, write a quick answer for these questions:

I could…

I should…

I might…

I will…

If you believe nothing can change then that is the way it will always be and nothing will change. Look at your answers. What's *really* stopping you?

Roberto Assagioli, founder of Psychosynthesis which is still being developed using his findings, says that two things are required to implement I can and I will. Ability which can be learned, and motivation, which is spirit. Stuart Miller interviewed Assagioli, and he talked about his time during the war when he was imprisoned by fascists. He chose acceptance and used

his time wisely. Read the article here.
http://www.psykosyntese.dk/a-196/

"Most people don't have that willingness to break bad habits. They have a lot of excuses and they talk like victims."

Carlos Santana

Re-cap. No excuses. If you want something in your life to change, only you have the power to make the change.

2 - Tell the Truth

Do you sometimes feel obligated to do what other people want you to do instead of doing what you want? Of course, in life it should be give and take, but the reality of it is that sometimes other people do all the taking and you end up doing things you'd rather not. The Toltec Indians lived by four agreements. The first, as depicted by Don Miguel Ruiz, was to be impeccable with your word.

"Speak with integrity. Say only what you mean."

Don Miguel Ruiz

Have you ever tried to make an excuse instead of blatantly telling the truth? An excuse, as we heard in the last chapter, is an opt out. How about learning to say what we want? Most people are too polite or too nice. I learned long ago that being nice and polite meant that people often put pressure on me to do things I wasn't keen on, and I was the one left feeling miserable.

No! It's such a small word, but carries so much power. Facing up to the truth will empower you and set you on the right track for peace of mind. Others may find your change of attitude hard to digest at first, but give them time. I heard a saying, *"those who mind do not matter and those who matter do not mind."* I believe this saying is attributed to Dr Seuss without citation of specific work. It's one of the phrases I find myself coming back to so often.

I have a friend who finds 'no' so difficult to say. However, she advises her children to follow my principles. This is a typical example of how her conversations go. 'I am going to start saying no, but half the time I don't really mind helping out,' she says trying to convince herself after she's spent the past ten minutes complaining about something she doesn't want to do. Some people will have no intention of changing, but are happy to go on complaining.

Of course, I am not suggesting that anyone should become selfish. It's good to help others and that is what makes the world go around. Giving help to others empowers you and you feel good. What I am advocating is saying no to things that make you feel discontent. If you are going to spend the rest of your day berating yourself for agreeing to something, was it worth it? If you had the chance would you turn it around and tell the truth? If not, then let it go and feel confident with the decision you made. However, if you regret the decision, life is too short for regrets. Learn by your mistakes. Either retract your agreement or make a pact with yourself that next time you'll tell the truth. The only stipulation is that you stick to your decision and feel good about it.

If you find yourself making snap decisions that leave you feeling bad, learn to ask for some time to think. *I'm not sure if I can do that, I'll let you know. I'm not sure I want to do that, I'll have a think and get back to you. I'm going to say no, if I change my mind I'll be in touch.*

When you tell the truth about how you feel, you are being honest with yourself and you have taken another step towards peace of mind. It doesn't matter what you choose to do, or not to do, but what does matter is that you feel good about yourself. You matter, always keep that at the forefront of your mind.

"No legacy is so rich as honesty."

William Shakespeare

Re-cap. Be honest, and be happy with your decisions.

3 - Let it go

We all have a past. Things we remember fondly, good times we'd like to relive, and then there's those other moments which seem to rear their ugly heads and haunt us. Amongst plenty of events we've been hurt, humiliated, embarrassed and lied to. We feel wronged. But you know what? They've gone! They are firmly in the past and you need to let go. No one can change what has gone and that's just where it is, *gone*. So now is the time to move on. Have that thought, bag it up and throw it away with the other rubbish. Or are you wanting to absorb yourself in self-pity for a while longer? It's fine to wallow – for a while!

What if your wallowing goes on too long and drags you down? Then it's time to pick yourself up, dust yourself off, and let it go. Easier said than done I hear you say. And you're right! But you have a choice. Only you can change the situation. You need to understand that people don't often admit when they're wrong and they're not going to admit to anything just to make you feel better. Dale Carnegie quotes Lord Chesterfield saying, *"Be wiser than other people if you can; but do not tell them so."*

A client of mine had an argument with her husband and was hurt by some of the things he said. By way of an apology, he said he was sorry she'd been hurt by what he said. He was surprised that another row ensued. My friend wanted him to retract what he'd said, and admit he was out of order. He couldn't see her problem and certainly wasn't going to go back on his beliefs.

I listened as she recounted the events. I asked her how she'd have felt if he'd apologised because she'd asked him to. Better, she answered, at least he'd have been really sorry. I had to disagree. Would he have been sorry, or would he have just been saying what she wanted to hear? Surely only an apology that came from the heart would suffice and have true meaning. She thought for a moment and then agreed that it's no good trying to force people to agree; they have to agree from their perspective, not yours.

I asked her to think for a moment about what he had said in the original argument. Had she been hurt by the truth or the injustice? Was he wrong, or did he believe what he said?

The old saying of the truth hurting is true. But it can only hurt if you don't like what you hear. Are you agreeing there's something you'd like to change about yourself? By asking tough questions, we can see clearly.

Back to the task of letting go. You can argue your point, and some people like a good argument, but if it's going to make you feel bad, don't do it. Why argue if you know you're right? Take satisfaction that the other person knows no better.

If you have been treated unfairly, don't hang on to it. Turn it around. These times define who we are and with a positive approach they make us stronger. *"Some of us think that holding on makes us strong; but sometimes it is letting go."* Hermann Hesse.

You only have one life, live it to the full, the way you want to. You have the power to make a change. Don't dwell on the past and things you have no control over. If you can't do anything about it, move on and let it go. Concentrate on today, and what matters is your happiness.

Recap. Let go of bad feelings from the past. They happened, they weren't nice and they've gone. So let them go; it's only you holding onto them and only you who can let them go.

4 - Admit you're wrong

This is a tough one. We all like to be right, or at least we think we're right. And there lies the problem—we think we're right, and everyone else thinks they are right. So what is the answer?

You have the right to believe in whatever you want, but so does everyone else. We have a stalemate! However, with hindsight, sometimes deep down inside we know the decision we made was wrong. Okay, so we can't all be right all the time, so let it go. But what if you can't let go? Why is it that our minds won't move on and get over bad situations? We want to forget, but those thoughts keep niggling away.

If you let your stubbornness control what you do, then you will dwell in that place and if you're lucky, time might lessen your feelings. But how much time do you have to waste on bad feelings? None! Life is too short.

You have a choice and only you know your true feelings and how much the situation is impacting on your life. It's a choice of carrying on as you are, or doing something about it.

Admitting you're wrong can be as small as *'I may have been hasty: I think I spoke before my brain engaged: You could have a point.'* Believe me, when you admit you're wrong the floodgates open and you're free. The weight lifts, and even if you don't get your desired outcome, you will feel you made the effort and your inner mind will reward you. *"I will be the first to admit I am not perfect and I make mistakes."*

Alberto Gonzales

The main point is that you feel good about your decision. You are in control and taking a step in the right direction will empower you. Be honest with yourself first, do you want to admit you were wrong? Will the admission make you feel better? What are the consequences of staying quiet? Is staying quiet the easy option, or will you be brave enough to confront the truth and make a difference?

"Mistakes are always forgivable, if one has the courage to admit them."

Bruce Lee

Recap. Admitting you're wrong isn't easy, but the rewards can make all the difference to your inner self.

5 - Forgive

Forgiving doesn't mean you like or agree with what has happened, but it does mean you can let go of your destructive feelings. The world would be a wonderful place if there was no harm, no injustice, and no conflict. Unfortunately, the dream of ultimate peace will never happen.

When something happens and you want to shout out how wrong, how unjust and unfair people can be, who really listens? You do! Your sympathisers will agree, they'll back you up, and they'll offer advice. But what really happens? You feel justified and worthy of complaint, and to a certain extent it's good to get things off your chest, but if you keep demeaning others, the only person to suffer is you. People who put others down while trying to justify themselves are usually the most miserable people you will meet.

This is due to the torment from the inner self going over what people have said to fuel feelings of being wronged, and you're back to knowing you're right. So now what are you going to do? You have a choice, and yes, I know I'm repeating myself, but you alone can break out of the vicious circle and feel better.

Forgive! They know no better and you can't change the way other people are, you can only change yourself. The act of forgiveness is to give up resenting what has happened. Resentment is negative and can only restrict harmony in your soul. When we hold on to negativity, we live in a bubble of resentment that is emotionally draining.

I am not a particularly religious person, but I do believe that karma and forgiveness go together. If you only believe in karma, then you leave no room for forgiveness. To uphold the belief that if someone has wronged they will be repaid accordingly can affect your peace of mind. These kind of thoughts can hold you back whereas forgiving will empower your self-esteem.

Truly forgive, and free yourself from torment. No excuses, you can do this for yourself. Be strong and be committed to your decision.

As you read, you can see a consistent theme of letting things go, and creating a more positive outlook being the key to making the changes you want. All these small changes will alter your self-esteem and you will find other people will respond to you with positivity. You are in a win-win place in your life and it can only get better. Believe in yourself.

"The weak can never forgive. Forgiveness is the attribute of the strong."

Mahatma Ghandi

Re-cap. Forgive others for your own well-being and peace of mind.

6 - Positive thinking

Years ago when I taught at an infant school, there was a big initiative on positive thinking. We had to say *please walk* instead of *don't run*. A simple enough change, but one that required a lot of thought. I hadn't even realised that the statements I made daily were negative. It's easy to get into the habit of negative thoughts, but once you begin to challenge yourself, the positive thoughts come easily.

Someone once told me I was the only person they knew who could take a dire situation and come up with something positive. This statement got me thinking about how some people don't even try to find anything positive to say or do. Is it that it's too easy to moan or put up with things rather than look for the good, or maybe it's just the habit of having a defeatist attitude?

Turn those thoughts around. Take stock of what you have instead of what you haven't. Find something to feel good about and appreciate what you have. You have already chosen to read this book, therefore you realise that things are not as good as they could be. But are you ready to open your mind to new opportunities?

Positivity is about seizing the moment. It's about picking yourself up, dusting down and blowing away the cobwebs. And yes, even positive people have cobwebs that need clearing out now and again.

So how can you do this? By making the journey, and every journey begins with the first step. Only you know what you want, or need to change to make things better for you, and that's where you need to start.

Commit to a challenge of being positive and focus on that one change. Give yourself a time when you will assess if you met your challenge. It could be as short as an hour or a day when you will commit to making a difference. If you reach the allotted time and you haven't quite reached your target – stay positive and extend the target time. Only giving up would be negative. Even if you decide you took on too much to begin with and back track with smaller steps, you are still heading towards your goal. If an hour is too long then cut the time, but be realistic; if it doesn't take you out of your comfort zone, then you're not going to make progress.

Get into the habit of starting your day with a positive outlook. What inspires you to feel good? A picture, a photograph sparking good memories, a flower – I love the way fragrance from a flower makes me feel. Whatever it is that that wakes up your senses, do it!

Make a positive plan for your day ahead. Something to look forward to. Maybe a walk, making a phone call, listening to some music, or something you haven't done for a while, but really enjoy. It's all about making yourself feel good and installing a positive attitude for the day ahead.

At the end of each day, think about what went well. If things could have been better, what can you do to turn it around tomorrow?

"Today is life - the only life you are sure of. Make the most of today. Get interested in something. Shake yourself awake."

Dale Carnegie

Recap. Keep your thoughts positive. Find something positive to do each day. Set a target and work towards it. You can change – you will change.

End of part 1

Part 2 - The new you!

By now you should have got a few gremlins out of the way who have been hampering your road to happiness and peace of mind. Don't worry if you're still working towards your goals, this isn't an overnight thing that's going to miraculously disappear. You've taken years of practice to get where you are, and so in all honesty, it's going to take time to make the changes.

Part 2 is all about a new outlook. Making small changes and taking short steps to discovering a new you. If a little doubt creeps in here and there, challenge it. If that condescending voice tells you nothing will change, and you'll always be the way you are, or if it tells you, *you can't*... you shout right back and tell those thoughts right where to get off! Some people find it helpful to look in the mirror and challenge their inner voice. For me, when I look in the mirror for a chat, I just laugh at myself, which does have a brilliant effect of making me realise how unimportant the negative thoughts really are. They are trying to drag you down—they need kicking into place—and they have no right to try to spoil your day, so don't let them get away with it.

Hold your head high and introduce yourself to the person you want to be.

7 - Find your happiness

What inspires you? I'm hoping that I can throw inspiration your way as you read, but what else motivates you, what inspires you to want to do something?

Someone I know, went home and began planning for building work for an extra bedroom he'd been talking about for years, just because he saw how one of his friends had transformed his place in a short space of time.

Another acquaintance rescued a puppy, and was inspired to get involved with animal welfare campaigning.

Inspiration can come from nowhere at the most unexpected times. It can leap out and grab us any time, any place. The problem is that these random acts of inspiration can't be planned. We don't know what will inspire us or when.

The good news is that, to a certain extent, we can inspire our mind to enjoy something. We all have personal triggers. Triggers that can instigate happiness.

Exercise: Make a list of ten things you like to do that make you happy. Maybe there are more than ten.

Mine would have to be: walking my dogs, playing with my cats, eating chocolate, drinking Lambrusco, writing, chatting with my friends, listening to rock and roll, dancing, paddling in waves, seeing stars, and taking a leisurely ride on the Harley. That last one will please my husband— we don't get out on the Harley as much as we'd like to. Just realised I have eleven on my list. Mmm—which one to take off? And that is the whole point of this exercise. When was the last time I paddled or looked up at the stars? Have you ever found the Milky Way on a clear night and then looked again through a pair of binoculars? It's stunning.

So now let's focus on the list. I eat chocolate quite often, so although it makes me happy, I'm quite used to it. So I'm going to add looking at some old photos and recalling some wonderful memories. I love doing that, but sort of forget to do it very often. Now do you get the idea? You're making this into a list of feel good, inspiring things to do that are right on your doorstep. If you have either more or less than ten, go with it!

Someone I know loves to declutter and feels liberated after turning out a cupboard she hasn't touched for ages. Afterwards she takes all the unwanted items to the charity shop, so she has a double feel-good factor. Marie Kondo has written a book on the subject. *The life-changing magic of tidying: A simple, effective way to banish clutter forever.* She advocates de-cluttering to help sort out your mind at the same time as your possessions. It seems to work for a lot of people, although I wouldn't be happy to de-clutter to the extent she advises. That is why I call this a personal trigger list. It's special to you, things that make you feel good.

Let's take this one step further. Is there something from your list you could choose to do every day? Listening to one piece of music, looking at some photos, reading, painting, drawing, walking, talking, singing, dancing etc. The list can be endless, but all the things *you* love to do. No excuses—everyone has things they like to do. Make the time for just one thing for you, each day.

The evening before or first thing in the morning, plan which one you will do and then you have something to look forward to. Make every day special— you deserve it.

If there are things on your list that aren't possible to do straight away, start a plan to lead towards your goal. Maybe that paddle in the sea is miles away. When could you go? How would you get there? Do you need to start saving towards the trip?

This is one of my favourite chapters. All about enjoying what we love; things that are often within our reach, but we ignore, or neglect to enjoy them as often as we could.

"The trick is to feel good for no reason."

Richard Bandler

Re-cap. Make a list of things you like to do and do one every day. Add to the list as you go. Have a plan and stick to it!

8 - Be who you want to be

Who are you? If you had to choose three words to describe yourself (without being too harsh) what would they be? Be honest and write them down. Now think of someone you know who appears to have everything going for them. Maybe someone you admire. Write down three words to describe them.

Now look at the two lists of words and compare them. Which set of words would you rather use to describe yourself? Maybe neither. Now think of and write down three words to describe the person you would like to be. Give this a bit of thought. Ask yourself why you would like to be the person described.

Did you know that many people have a public face? A face for the outside world to see. Of course you knew that; chances are that you put on your public face now and again. But the main point here is that *you're* deciding when to put on that public face.

How do you feel when you put on your public face and pretend all's well? For a length of time you feel better. You chat, laugh, listen and enter into a sociable occasion because that's how you want to be seen—hence it's your public face, the one people see.

Even if you only lift yourself up a fraction, even if it's only for a short space of time, you've given yourself a break. Why do these breaks have to be for other people? Why can't you give yourself a break now and again?

You have the power to decide on the way you want to be. In the previous chapter we talked about things that inspire you and things you like to do. I suggested doing one thing each day and that's a great starting point, but you don't have to stop there. Be who you want to be!

What small steps could you take to becoming the new you? Look at the positive people around you, and take a leaf from their book. Become an actor/actress for a while and see how it feels. If you're laughing or mocking me at this point, brilliant! I have a reaction. Go for it! You will feel better and that is what life is all about; being the person you want to be.

Don't make excuses before you try something new. You're reading this to make changes; take a step forward and do a bit of acting. If nothing else it will lift your spirits, and if you lift your spirits, you're heading in the right direction.

"Live today with gusto."

Dale Carnegie

Recap. Act like the person you want to be, and become that person.

9 - Small steps

How often have you set yourself a goal and failed? Then you're left feeling frustrated and despondent. You made a choice to do something you wanted to do, or felt you should do, so why was it so hard to see the mission through, and succeed?

Perhaps you weren't dedicated, or maybe you fooled yourself into believing it was what you wanted. We set ourselves up for failure in many ways. Sometimes we jump into something that seems like a good idea, only to find out it was someone else's dream, but wasn't what *we* were really wanting to do.

By this I mean it's easy to hear someone's plan and think it's what you'd like to do. We all need inspiration and it's good to get that from anywhere, but always take time to consider if the task you're setting yourself is really what *you* want. You always have to take on a challenge for *you*.

Why is it that some people seem to succeed at all they do, while others never seem to quite hit the mark? Are some people born lucky or do they have a gift that ensures their success? Maybe they were fortunate enough to make the right choices, or maybe they know a secret we'd all love to share.

If there is a secret, I believe it's the way we tackle a challenge that leads us to failure or success. I know of two men who had great plans for setting up their own businesses.

One began small by hiring the cheapest premises, did most of the work himself and gradually built up his profession to a large, profitable company. He took a small step at a time and reached his goal.

The second man was up for a challenge and jumped right in at the deep end. He hired staff, rented impressive offices and leased himself a company car. With all of this were overheads he couldn't sustain for very long, and soon he struggled to pay his bills. Despite the difficulties he also reached his goal.

Look at these examples and think about quality of life.

The first man took great pride each step of the way and celebrated every achievement which moved him closer to his successful business.

The second man didn't have time to celebrate. He had sleepless nights as he strived to keep his business from sinking.

Who would you rather be? Both, no doubt, had worries and issues to overcome along the way, but by taking the slower pace the first man had time to enjoy the experience.

Some people have to barge along in life, chasing a dream, and they just don't realise that their dream can be fulfilled in a much nicer way.

Wayne Dyer made a wonderful video on this subject. Go and take a look. The Shift by Wayne Dyer – Positive Attitude. He talks a lot of sense about putting happiness first and not giving up your peace of mind to chase a relationship, money or something you think you need and don't. It's all about taking things in your stride and staying happy on life's journey.

www.youtube.com/watch?v=yfT8Ts6wPFs

By taking small steps, you can enjoy the journey. Every path taken has to start with a step. Take your step, but don't worry about the destination.

"Life was never meant to be a struggle. Everything is out there waiting for you."

Stuart Wilde

Re-cap. A little at a time will empower you with positivity to accomplish your dream.

10 - Blow away the cobwebs

We've all got a few cobwebs we'd like to be rid of. Those pesky thoughts that keep popping in to remind us of things we'd rather put behind us or at least forget about for a while.

Routines can hold you back from moving on, whereas something new can revive your senses and make you feel alive. When was the last time you did something out of the ordinary?

If you always take the same route, it's likely there will be nothing much to capture your attention. You will have seen it all before and therefore you pass by in the same state of mind as every other time.

Do you ever walk instead of taking the car? A good walk will revive all your senses, and to walk a new route will awaken your curiosity. Look around you. Look up. Look across the road.

A colleague of mine used to cycle to work. I loved hearing tales of her journey and soon realised that jumping into my car each morning was so boring. I saw nothing. I hadn't ridden a bike for years, in fact since my cycling to school days, and felt pretty certain that I wouldn't be able to keep my balance. I borrowed an old bike from a friend and set off on a very wobbly ride along a quiet road. After less than a minute, I found myself smiling. I felt wonderful. The wind against my face, with my legs now peddling faster, I was on top of the world. A definite head out of the window moment!

I didn't always cycle to work, but when I did, my days seemed to begin with a purpose. I had more energy, felt happier and got much more done than when I took the car. The strange thing was that when I arrived back home in the evenings, I had the energy to carry on instead of sinking into an armchair with a cup of tea.

Of course, cycling isn't an option for everyone, but just getting out there and blowing away a few cobwebs will inspire and energise you. Could you go and see a park you haven't been to in a while? Visit a local area you haven't visited for ages? Hop on a bus to a neighbouring town? Go to a swimming pool or nature area? The list is endless, but there is something different out there for everyone, you just need to do it!

Often habits are helpful, but some can also become a bore, like taking the same route. There is a wonderful

Spanish proverb: habits begin as cobwebs and end up as chains.

What will you do today? How many cobwebs will you blow away? No excuses.

"I can't change the direction of the wind, but I can adjust my sails to always reach my destination."

Jimmy Dean

Re-cap. Do something different today.

11 - Wake up earlier

When you're not feeling 100% good, it's not easy to get going in the morning. Pulling up the covers and keeping your eyes shut from the world is much more tempting. Maybe you're not sleeping too well and need all the rest you can get.

Now you're going to think I've completely lost the plot. I'm going to suggest that you get up earlier than you need to. Set your alarm for half-an-hour earlier and give yourself time to enjoy the start of your day.

There is nothing worse than getting out of bed and rushing around. Believe me, I know. Every minute used to count as I pulled on clothes, back to front, in my rush to be out of the door in time. By the time I arrived, wherever I was going, I'd be feeling quite stressed and then continued to play catch-up until I settled down and could take a breath.

When someone suggested I set the alarm earlier, I couldn't see the point. I never arrived anywhere late, so why get up earlier than I needed to? Just try it for one week, I was urged.

If I'm honest, I think I took the challenge to prove to myself that nothing would change, except I'd lose an extra half-an-hour of valuable rest time. The first day, I was nearly late. I had so much time on my hands I forgot to keep an eye on the clock. The second day, I took things in my stride and popped on the radio. The top of the hour beeps kept me focused on the time. I had plenty of time to take the pretty route to work and arrived ten minutes early. I made myself a drink and felt at ease. Mmm! This relaxed feeling must be a one-off. Not so! My week got better as I transformed into a calm human being who had time to enjoy the start of each day. Gone had the neurotic lunatic trying to calm down from a frenzied beginning.

Nowadays, I get up an hour before I have to and walk the dogs before I do anything else. When you give yourself time, it can only have a good effect. Even if you haven't got anywhere to rush off to, getting up early will set your day off to a good start. You will have a positive beginning, and every day should start like that.

A small habit of lying in bed too long will make you lethargic for the day, whereas getting up with a plan will inspire you and give you time to do something nice.

"My favourite things in life don't cost any money. It's really clear that the

most precious resource we all have is time."

Steve Jobs

Re-cap. Get up earlier and jump-start your day. You won't have this day again, so don't waste it lounging around in bed.

12 - Talk yourself into something good

You're getting up earlier, and now is the time to set your day off to a good start. How often do you talk to yourself? Okay, I've let the cat out of the bag—here goes! I talk to myself all the time. I also talk continuously to my animals, but that's for another day.

Anyone who doesn't admit to talking to themselves, needs to think again. Everyone talks to themselves in their head. They moan about what's wrong with the world, they put it to rights when they can, and they're quite happy with that. They tell themselves something and they believe what they say. You are talking to yourself all day long. Whether you believe it or not, these are affirmations.

What about when things go wrong? You drop, break or spill something, and berate yourself out loud, even if there's no one else around to hear you. You believe you are the idiot that you just called yourself.

You also believe in all the things that are holding you back. All the baggage stopping you from living the life you want. You believe all the negative things about the way you are. Why do you believe it? Because it's what you keep telling yourself, and you've rammed it into your brain so often that you have yourself believing it's true.

It doesn't have to be like that. If you've talked yourself into these negative beliefs, you can just as easily talk yourself out of them.

Go to the mirror. Right now! Wherever you are, look in the mirror. If you're on the tube or driving, then do this as soon as you can, but don't skip past this and forget to do this important step.

Look in the mirror. Is that the person you want to be looking back at you? Now pull back your shoulders, and straighten up. Now smile. A happy smile. You might need to practise this if you haven't had a lot to smile about recently. Go on, smile again.

Now I want you to say "I can do this. I will do this." Now say it like you believe it. You need to believe you can do this. You are the only person who can do this for *you*. Shout it out! "I can do this. I will do this!" Okay, now we're all in the same place and it's a good place to be.

Now think of something you want for your day. For example: 'My day will be fantastic.' I will be strong.' I will hold my head up high.' 'I am going to succeed.' This has to be something you want for your day. You can have the same saying for every day, but you have to believe you are going to achieve a positive outcome. Throughout the day, keep telling yourself the same sentence. It's not going to cost you anything, not even time. It doesn't matter if you say it in your head or out aloud. Just say it!

Do you know what will happen? You are going to start believing what you say. This really does work. You are going to make a small step forward to believing in yourself, and that is one step further than yesterday. You made a promise when we began our journey, a promise to yourself, and now you are going to begin to reap the benefits.

Listen to yourself and believe.

"Very little is needed to make a happy life; it is all within yourself, in your way of thinking."

Marcus Aurelius

Re-cap. Have a saying for the day and keep it in your mind all day. Hold your head up, your shoulders back, and smile.

I've put together a few simple affirmations that you might find helpful. I would suggest you add affirmations that are personal to you.

I choose to be happy

I love life

I can change if I choose to

I am going to enjoy every moment of my day

My future looks good

I am kind

I am happy

Today is a new beginning

I trust in myself

I have the power to choose

I will never give up

I have a choice about how I survive conflicts

I will only have positive thoughts

I am grateful

I'm going to commit to a new me

I can

I will

13 - Understand your triggers

We all have habits, rituals that we follow day in, and day out, without much thought. Our rituals don't need much thought because they're things we do all the time. We're in the habit of following a routine and it's easy to wallow in what we know or do regularly.

Have you ever wondered why your day can start with you feeling on top of the world and then for no apparent reason something changes and you feel defeated and at a loss?

So what are you going to do? Are you going to stick with how you feel or are you prepared to turn things around? You could beat yourself up with negative affirmations, *I knew I'd feel bad, I knew it wouldn't last, this is just me, I'm never happy for long.*

Remember the last chapter? If you tell yourself often enough you will believe it.

The first thing to do is try to find something that might be triggering your feelings. Ask yourself where you were. What you were doing? When did things change? Who were you with? What were you thinking about? Was there a reason for a change of mood? What brought on the change? Did you allow a negative thought to slip in and spoil your day? There's usually something you can identify if you dig deep enough and are honest with yourself.

Understanding your triggers is the key to changing them. Once you have identified a trigger you can begin to focus on making changes. You can avoid things that are diverting your path to happiness.

You can control your own thoughts; don't let your thoughts control you, because that's what you're allowing to happen if you let your thoughts get you down.

If your trigger turns out to be a result of someone else's actions, you have a choice about how you react. No one can get you down if you don't let them. Obviously, I don't know your trigger or how you feel, but you do, and you can turn it around. You have a choice, and no one has the right to spoil your day. You cannot change anyone else, but you can choose to have the thought, and then let it go.

"It is best to avoid people and situations that you know drive you crazy."

Stuart Wilde

Recap. Find your triggers and avoid them.

14 - Choose your friends

Most of us have people in our lives who make us feel good. We spend some time with them and we feel refreshed. We also have people who drain us emotionally. I'm not suggesting you drop all the people in your life who don't make you feel good, but you can turn things around.

Ask yourself why you feel like you do after you've spent time with certain people. The people who inspire you are easy to spend time with. They're the people who have positive energy and pass those feelings on to you. When you're with those people, you can be anywhere and have a good time. You come away wanting to spend more time with them.

Then there are the friends or family you walk away from, feeling weary.

These are the ones with negative energy and that too, can rub off onto you. They rob you of your energy.

Once again you have a choice. You can see less of negative people and spend most of your time with friends who make you feel good. Here she goes again! Easier said than done, you cry.

Okay, so there are some people who zap our energy, but they are still an important part of our lives. Take a moment to think about the time you spend with these people. Why do they have a negative effect on you? Do you somehow feed their negativity and even encourage it by being a sitting target? Do you find yourself agreeing with them for an easy life?

Can you meet with these people in a different environment and therefore have something new to discuss and chat about? Can you turn their negativity around and give them something positive to dwell on? There must be some way, if you really have to have these people in your life, to change the direction. Maybe it would even be possible for you to help them to think positively, after all, it's something you've learned to do. Tell them how much better you feel.

Keep your attitude positive, remember, people can only zap your energy if you let them, and you have a choice. Keep the power zappers at a distance you can handle. This is all about you and you have decided to make some changes to get yourself to where you want to be. Don't allow anyone to make your journey difficult.

"Surround yourself with positive people and you'll be a positive person."

Kellie Pickler

"If you surround yourself with love and the right people, anything is possible."

Adam Green

Recap: See less of people who drain your energy. See more of people who make you feel good.

Author note

How are you doing?

If you've read this far and tried a few things, well done! I hope you're getting along okay and are finding my suggestions helpful. (If that's you, then skip the rest of this page and move on to chapter 15.)

I'm hoping that no one is needing to read this next bit, but here goes! Have you tried any of the strategies I've suggested? Maybe you're going to read to the end, and then start trying a few things. Or perhaps you'll read to the end, close the last page and forget what you've read.

How serious are you about wanting to change? If you've read this far, and haven't tried anything, then I am going to stick my neck out here and say that you're wasting time. Okay, those of you who like to read through a book to get the feel and then re-read to implement, I'm not including you; as long as you are really going to stick by that.

But, there will be some of you that plan to try everything, but won't ever quite make it happen. Well, what are you waiting for? Nothing is going to happen tomorrow, if you don't take the first step today.

The ideas I've presented are mostly changes you can make to start the ball rolling and make a difference to your life. You only get one shot at life, and it's worth making the most of every moment. Time is precious.

If you've tried a few suggestions and nothing seems to be helping, please keep going. With a positive attitude, things will turn around. We're all different, and these things take time.

All the reading, understanding, agreement and intention is not going make a difference if you don't apply what you've learned.

So don't wait; do something now!

15 - Feeling Good

We're constantly told about the latest evidence, and what we should be doing to stay healthy. I'm no expert on health. In fact, I eat chocolate, drink wine, and love a Danish pastry. So, now you know I'm not a health fanatic, but I do believe (and there are plenty of studies about this) that what we eat can affect the way we feel.

I'm not talking about diets, and healthy eating programmes, I'm talking about everything in moderation, and making a life change. As I said, I'm no expert, and there's a lot of help out there from people who are.

What I'm suggesting, following the theme of what we've already talked about, is small changes that can make a difference to the way we feel. There are certain things that can impact on our well-being and that includes the mind.

A poor diet is one of the main contributing factors that can make you feel tired, and have a lack of energy. Take some time here to think about your diet. Be honest. If your body isn't getting what it needs to function properly, then how can it work to its full capacity for you? The Mental Health Foundation reports that evidence suggests that good nutrition is essential for our mental health. Follow the link to find out more.

www.mentalhealth.org.uk/a-to-z/d/diet-and-mental-health

Are you exercising? I'm not talking about joining the gym, although some of you might want to or already do that. I'm talking about taking the stairs instead of the lift. Walking a short distance instead of taking the car.

Do you get enough fresh air? Open the window and breathe it in. If you live in a built up area, walk to the nearest park.

Do you rest enough? Work, rest, and play (isn't that what the popular ad said?) Our bodies need rest, just as much as they need to work and play. Everything in moderation, and it's all important for your well-being.

Do you drink enough water? Stress, anxiety and feeling under the weather can be attributed to toxins in your body. Drinking plenty of water can flush toxins out. Water also improves your energy levels and has hidden powers of having a positive effect on mood swings and headaches. Experts suggest we should be drinking 8 – 10 glasses every day. Follow the link and find out more.

www.healthy-holistic-living.com/2-ways-water-improves-mental-health.html

I can't stress how important it is to have a healthy eating and drinking lifestyle, with regard to feeling good. Basically, if you put rubbish in, you're going to get rubbish out, and that's putting it politely.

Recap: Drink more water and change a few eating habits to make yourself feel good from the inside.

16 - Make a list

As silly as it sounds, it took me a long time to realise the benefits of a list. Of course, I'd written shopping lists and had a slim-line calendar to help keep track of daily appointments, but it wasn't until I committed to a list that things started to change.

I used to spend a lot of time rebuking myself for not accomplishing as much as I wanted to in a day. I'd start out with great plans and then gradually as the day went on, half of the good intentions got lost and disappeared into insignificance. That left me feeling like I'd failed and it wasn't a good feeling.

Then I began to write a list of things I wanted to do in the course of my day. This can be at home and at work. Once I had a plan, I prioritised which made sure the important stuff got done first. I ticked off each task as it was accomplished. Guess what? Those ticks had some sort of magical power over my mind-set. They pushed me on to finish another task so I could gradually get through the list. The knock-on effect was that I worked faster and was more dedicated, as though on a mission. This also made me aim for perfection. I could only tick when a job was finished, and finished properly or it'd be cheating. Seriously? Yes!

If you only put in half the effort you're only going to achieve half the outcome. The only person you let down is yourself by not doing your best.

The overall effect was astounding. Through doing nothing more than a list and a few ticks, my days suddenly turned positive. I was reaching my targets and beyond, and I felt proud I'd succeeded.

It might be a small achievement but it made me realise how small steps can make a difference. By prioritising, the important tasks were done and if at the end of the day there were tasks not accomplished they could move to the next day. If I had to move the same task twice, it went to the top of the list on the third day and had to be done first.

Silly rules, but they motivated me and made a difference. You'll know what works for you.

Your working day might not be the same as mine, and you might be thinking this chapter isn't going to work for you. But have a look at other areas of your life. Are there letters you've been putting off writing, or emails to send or reply to? Sometimes it's easy to put off what we don't want to do, or simply can't be bothered to do. You know what? Tasks hanging around on the, *I must do that* mind list, hang there and nag at you.

Try it! Write those chores and things you've been not wanting to do on a list and start working on them. You'll feel good to have them out of the way and when you wake tomorrow it'll be one less thing to think about.

"I love the ritual of drawing up lists, and there's something wonderfully satisfying about ticking tasks off."
Shaida Kazie Ali

Recap: Write a list and tick off the tasks as you accomplish them. Break free from your nagging mind!

17 - How are you doing?

By now you have read a few ideas about taking small steps towards a happier life. Have you looked at your checklist? How are you doing? Not everything I suggest will benefit everyone, and you have to choose what makes a difference to you. Someone once told me *you live the life*. I admit at the time I didn't know what they were talking about, but now I know it's my outlook that makes all the difference.

I've had tough times. At one point my mind went into severe lock-down. I knew the dire situation I faced could never be resolved, and for me there would be no happy outcome. After the awful event, I gave myself time to reflect on what had happened and what, if anything, I could have done differently to change the outcome. What if…

You know what? No matter how long and hard I thought about the situation, there were numerous outcomes and scenarios, but in reality, the situation was beyond my control and I did the best I could. One day I'm going to write a book and reveal my secret trauma, but until then, it's stored away and not allowed to impact on my life today. That time has had its day and is history.

Why am I telling you this? Because, I could have let events ruin what I had. I could have let something inside me die. But I didn't. I faced the challenge and, despite the sadness, I grew determined to move on. How did I do that? By implementing the strategies I'm now sharing with you.

I could have just shared my ideas, but I want you to know that life hasn't always been kind to me. I've had my fair share of knocks, but I found a determination to stay on top and be a survivor.

I made choices, and that's what you need to do. I want you to look at life from a new perspective. I want you to open your eyes and begin to live the life you want.

So, have you been consistent? Have you made the commitment and began to reap the benefits? Are you being positive? Have you blown away the cobwebs? Are you doing the things that make you happy? Have you found your triggers and dismissed people who don't make you feel good?

I hope you read this book several times and take from it the best you can to make the difference you want for yourself.

There will always be the non-believers. The people who refuse to try and make a difference. I would say to them that they are always going to be where they are today because they are too stuck in their ways to move forward and give something their best shot.

"If you do what you've always done, you'll get what you've always gotten."
Anthony Robbins

Stand tall and know you can do this.

"Choosing to be positive and having a grateful attitude is going to determine how you're going to live your life."
Joel Osteen

Recap: Take a look at what small steps you have already made. Promise yourself that above all else you will try to make a difference. Be determined!

18 - Take a moment to choose

Are you in a rut? A rut in your relationship, your life, your job? Do your days roll into one another with the same old annoyances winding you up, and making you discontent?

When was the last time you took a step back and really assessed what's happening? Sometimes it's easy to go along with the usual and not question what we want. Do you put up with situations because it's the lazy, easier option?

Just because it's the way someone else is, or the way it's always been, doesn't mean you have to stick with what makes you cringe and feel discontent.

I'm not suggesting that you start trying to change anyone else; that's a non-starter. You already know that you can only change the choices you make which can then have an impact on others.

How about taking a moment to consider your choices? Choose to choose!

Do you have to respond when someone or something antagonises you? No you don't. You have a choice. Find a new way around the situation. Nothing in life is cast in stone.

An acquaintance bemoaned the fact that her husband was a night person, whereas she was a morning person. Staying up late always had an impact the following morning, and the woman felt that her days were lost to tiredness and feeling lethargic. I asked her why she couldn't go to bed earlier than her husband. She said he wouldn't like it. I put the point to her that staying up late was his choice, and going to bed early was her choice. They could both choose, why would there be a problem?

She took the advice on board and went to bed early twice before her husband switched off the television and joined her with an early night. The following night, feeling energised after a few early nights, she stayed up late with him. A simple solution to a problem that wasn't really a problem, but a situation that niggled away day after day, leading to disgruntlement.

You have to be strong enough to take a moment to think things through, and without being argumentative or provoking a dispute, make choices in your life.

I'm not suggesting being selfish and wanting things all your own way. For any relationship to be successful, at home or work, there has to be give and take, but you have the right to choose to change the way things have always been and reach a compromise. Sometimes a talk can smooth the way.

"Strategy is about making choices, trade-offs; it's about deliberately choosing to be different."

Michael Porter

Recap: Instead of going along with the norm and feeling irritated, choose to choose.

19 - Open your world

In an earlier chapter I encouraged you to say *no* to things you didn't want to do. I said you should put what you want first. As I said, it's hard to say no when people expect you to always be there for them. But there's another time when we say *no* all too easily,

No! It's an easy word that seems to slip in all over the place without too much thought. How much thought do we give anything before we say no?

I worked in Bubble and Squeak pre-school with Caroline, the manager. We had an activity plan we followed each session and the group ran smoothly.

One morning she arrived with a new strategy. We couldn't say *no* to something a child wanted to do, without a good reason. At home, her daughter had told her that she always said no, and it wasn't fair. That small statement changed her thinking.

The nursery still ran smoothly, but with more open-mindedness from the staff, the children were content. The strategy of child centred learning is now used in schools all over the world.

In our adult lives we think we know what's best, and we like to follow routines. For a moment, think about opening your mind to other people's suggestions. Instead of saying an immediate *no*, give the suggestion some thought and ask yourself *why*.

Why? Why do we say no without any good reason? Do new ideas challenge your comfort zone? Or is it because we think we only like doing the same things we've always done? None of these are good reasons!

I bet you've raised your eyebrows at some of the things I've suggested; be honest, I bet you have! But you know what? It doesn't matter to my life whether you try my suggestions or not, but it does matter to yours. Actually, it does matter to me if you try my suggestions. I want you to know how good life can be, and if you don't even try, I've wasted my time.

Taking on board new ideas could make all the difference to your life. Even if you only try something once, you have a fifty-fifty chance of enjoying it. How will you know if you missed out on something fantastic, if you always say no?

Be honest. You owe yourself that much. Have you given ideas and suggestions enough thought before saying no?

Turn things around, and with a little bit of time and allowing your mind to open up to new ideas, you could find a whole new world out there waiting for you.

"It is in your moment of decision that your destiny is shaped."

Anthony Robbins

Recap: Stop before you say no and ask yourself why. Why are you really saying no, and is it a good enough reason?

20 - Just do it anyway!

There are no guarantees in life, only the certainty that one day will be our last. I sincerely hope not, but what if that day was tomorrow? What would you choose to do?

We all know the saying about not putting off until tomorrow… In the last chapter we talked about the why.

If you have something you want to do, a secret ambition, a hidden agenda, what are you waiting for? Just do it!

Why wait? What is really holding you back? Is there a little voice in your head telling you how silly you are?

When my mum came to stay, my husband told her about a motorbike trip we'd taken, around Portugal.

"I've always wanted to go on a Harley Davidson," she said.

Tim nodded. "I'll take you for a ride in the morning."

She laughed. "I'm eighty! I can't go on one now."

"Why?"

She opened her mouth and then closed it again.

I joined the conversation. "I'll be there to help you on and off. You'll love it."

Her eyes sparkled. "I'm going to do this!" She exhaled. "Bet I don't sleep tonight."

After her ride of a lifetime, she beamed for the rest of the day. The point is, she just did it! If an eighty-year-old can go on a Harley for the first time, what is it that you can't do?

You have to make a decision. You choose to do something and then you do it. Give yourself a moment to imagine what you would feel in the minutes after you've *done it*. Would you feel inspired, invigorated, happy, relieved? Only you will know the feeling of meeting the challenge.

Don't let others hold you back. If you have something that's been lingering in the background, release the passion. It's not about succeeding and being the best, it's about doing what you want. Giving it a go. You have nothing to lose, so do it!

"You must live in the present, launch yourself on every wave, find your eternity in each moment."
Henry David Thoreau

Recap: What is it you've always fancied having a go at? Don't keep it in the back of your mind: just do it! Live for the moment!

21 - Step out of your comfort zone

We all know people who take risks. We might think they are unwise (putting it politely) or we wonder why they want to jeopardise everything on a whim. I do agree that some people jump in with no fear of consequences, and they don't always come out unscathed.

Then there are people who have never taken a risk and stay secure in their comfort zone.

Stepping out of your comfort zone can be frightening. It can also be exhilarating and rewarding. Ask yourself, what is the worst that could happen? What is the best that could happen?

You don't have to do anything, or risk anything you're not happy with, but don't ever have regrets over something you did; only regret the things you never tried.

Trying something that doesn't work out the way you wanted it to can be attributed to a learning curve. We learn by our mistakes and move on. Mistakes make us what we are.

There is a saying—better to have tried and lost than to have caught your balls in a mangle! Don't even ask where that came from, but it's so true.

I took one of the biggest risks in my life on a man who lived up a mountain in Spain. That's another story, but I took a huge risk and never looked back.

I weighed up what I had, and what I had to lose. There were family concerns—would they forgive me? If they loved me, yes. My job—I could find another one. What if I wasn't happy—so leave! There were countless questions and for each one I found an answer. What if I hadn't taken the risk?

I wouldn't be writing this book on a Spanish hillside, feeling grateful to be gifted with such a happy life. I'd be wondering, what if?

I can't count the number of people who told me they couldn't have done what I did. Amongst other things, they described me as brave, reckless, strong, and wild. I don't see myself as any of those. I was just a lady, willing to take a chance and see how things worked out. In my eyes there is nothing brave, reckless, strong or wild about someone who takes a risk. If I'm honest, taking the challenge was scary and exciting at the same time.

I've also taken risks that haven't worked out so well, but I've learned to accept that things sometimes happen for a reason and I've moved on, putting it down to experience.

So if there's something you're considering, don't regret not knowing *what if.* Find out what you're missing by stepping out of your comfort zone. You might never look back.

   "Be willing to step outside your comfort zone once in a while; take the risks in life that seem worth taking. The ride might not be as predictable if you'd just planted your feet and stayed put, but it will be a heck of a lot more interesting."
                    Edward Whitacre, Jr.

   Recap: Weigh up *if I do* and *if I don't* outcomes. Have an easy back-up plan such as *I'll try something else* and go for it anyway.

22 - Walk tall

Have you ever watched confident people and taken notice of the way they carry themselves? They don't try to blend into the background, they walk tall, proud to be who they are.

Don't confuse loud or extrovert people for those with confidence. Personality doesn't make confidence. Confidence is trusting one's own abilities.

If you don't trust and believe in yourself, how can you expect others to believe in you? Self-confidence can be learned. It is how you see yourself, and nothing has to stay the way it is now.

Have you been practising your affirmations each day? If not go back and re-read chapter twelve. If you tell yourself something often enough, you will believe in yourself.

Pull back your shoulders, smile, and always make eye contact with the person you are talking to. Just these small changes will make you feel more confident and make you seem confident to others. If people think you are confident they will treat you accordingly, and that's a winning bonus for you. The way people respond to you can have a huge impact on your confidence.

Research shows that speaking slowly and clearly makes you feel confident. If you rush through what you have to say, people can't always take in what you're saying and you might receive a negative response. If you're clearly understood, people can take on board what you're saying and respond accordingly.

Dress in clothes that make you feel comfortable. If you wear something that makes you feel awkward, it's going to impact on your confidence. When you buy a new outfit, try wearing it at home and see if it sits well after a bit of time. Looking good—feeling good, it's all in the same category.

Looking presentable, including cleanliness, hair and shoes, will enhance your confidence. People like groomed, and people will treat you the way they perceive you.

If you have to take on a new task at work, find out all you can in advance. Knowing, even the basics, will stand you in good stead and stand you apart from the crowd. You don't have to understand everything, you just have to have made an effort and it will be rewarded.

So now you're looking good, feeling good, speaking slowly and clearly and you've got everyone's attention. Someone is going to pay you a compliment. Smile confidently and say thank you. Don't turn that positive energy into negativity, by disagreeing. If someone says you look nice, believe them! They didn't have to say it, they mean it! So thank them and feel good.

"I can live for two months on a good compliment."
Mark Twain

Recap: You are what you are telling yourself. Walk tall with shoulders back, a smile and make eye contact. Believe in yourself and others will follow.

23 - Your glass is always full

The saying of a glass half full or half empty is a popular way of describing positive or negative thinking. The pessimist will see his glass as half empty whereas the optimist's glass is always half full.

Research shows that being optimistic creates happiness, wealth and health. When we expect good things, we act in a way that brings positive results. Pessimism will stop you from doing the very things that might have turned things around.

No one's glass is really half empty; the top half is full of air! Having a full glass is a choice. There's always a pitcher or tap nearby to replenish the goods and that's the way to look at life.

If your focus is always on possessions, failures and moods, it's easy to forget to be thankful for what you have. You'll have so much more if you give it a bit of thought.

Write a list of things to be thankful for. I'll start you off with a few you might not think of. Friends, family, health, sight, weekends, pets, home, education, fresh air, time, water, love, speech, music, and above all, you woke up this morning. The list is endless.

Take time and keep adding to the list. Days out, special times, the ocean, reading, birds and so on.

It's so easy to hang on to what you haven't got, but you already have a lot more than a lot of other people in the world.

Put the list somewhere you can see it easily and keep looking at it and adding to it. Even a few coins in your pocket is more than some have.

Each time you add to the list you are filling your glass and your glass is going to stay full because you have so

113

much to be grateful for. Stay positive and optimistic and good things will come.

Opportunity comes to optimists, don't kill it with pessimism. Give yourself a chance at the good life and go get yourself a full glass.

"Some people grumble that roses have thorns; I am grateful that thorns have roses."
Alphonse Karr, A tour around my garden

Recap: Make a list of things to be thankful for.

24 - Life isn't a competition

At some point in our lives, we've all had someone we've looked up to. Maybe for you it's a friend, a neighbour or family member. It could be someone famous, rich, intelligent, good looking, or outgoing.

How do you know what they've really got? They might be financially rich, but are they rich inside?

I've given a few superficial suggestions of who some of you might aspire to be like. But we've all heard the saying be careful what you wish for.

Many people strive to be like someone else, or to have what others have. Stop! You don't really know what they've got. You don't know if they have self-confidence, peace of mind, or happiness. The only vision you have is from the outside.

Have you ever opened yourself up to the world and let everyone in? Mankind are much more likely to show the world the things they don't mind sharing. The uncomfortable bits are kept well hidden.

Take a look around and open your eyes to those you would never aspire to. They might be poor, ill, unhappy, sad, or maybe they just haven't read this book!

You know nothing more or less about either group of people so why do you want to be like them? Be yourself and be equal.

Everyone has flaws, but you will never know what anyone else's life is truly like. So stop comparing.

If you continuously compare to those who seemingly have more, you will feel a hopeless sense of pessimism. If you are someone who keeps comparing themselves to others, then start looking at those who are less well-off. I don't necessarily mean financially; I am referring to life as a whole. Compare what you have with those less fortunate.

All of this still comes back to not really knowing who is rich in life. I have known people, with few material possessions, who are content with their lot and have so much on the inside that they put a lot of us to shame.

I knew a homeless man (Paul) who left himself penniless to help someone else in need. He didn't let his situation embitter his faith in fellow man. He didn't wallow in jealousy, he made the most of what he had and managed to bring a smile to those who were lucky enough to meet and get to know him. People were so cruel to him; they knew no better. He was one man who influenced my life and opened my eyes. Another story for another day.

So don't spend and waste your life on a competition you won't win. Stop putting yourself through the despair of not having enough. Live life from the inside and give yourself the satisfaction of winning without even entering a competition.

"When you are content to be simply yourself and don't compare or compete, everybody will respect you."

Lao Tzu

Recap: Don't put others on a pedestal. Everyone has flaws in life; you just don't know what theirs are.

25 - Are you proud of yourself?

I hope you are. You are nearly at the end of the first book in the Choose to Change series. You've made me proud. You've read this far, so I feel proud of both of us. Me, for writing this book and attempting to make a difference, and you for sticking with it this far.

There will be a few people, still reading, who think nothing I've written relates to them. Go back and re-read chapter 2 about telling the truth! On the other hand, there are those who like having something to complain about, and they aren't ready to choose to change.

Others will be thinking there are a few ideas that have helped. You are the people I have written for. If anyone takes something I've suggested, puts it into practice and feels better for it, then my job is done.

For those of you who skipped through the book and didn't do the exercises, I suggest going back and slowing down. The ideas are meant to work with time, and gradually change your mind-set. If you hurried through hoping to gain everything I pledged, you will feel deflated.

I suggest everyone reads this book several times. Each time you look again, you'll find a snippet to carry you forward. Don't be a self-doubter. Be proud that you stuck at what you set out to do. Reward yourself!

Little treats can go a long way to making yourself feel good. Treats don't have to be expensive, just something you like will do you good. It could be a walk, a coffee, a chocolate, an hour of reading, listening to a favourite singer, window shopping, people watching, whatever rocks your boat! Just do it!

When you reward yourself, you'll know you've accomplished something, and even the smallest step in the right direction makes all the difference. Be honest and only take a reward when you reach the next destination. Set yourself small, manageable goals and have a reward set up for when you get where you want. A long, or unreachable goal will seem like a huge challenge, but still set that goal and have a wonderful treat in mind. Along the way, working towards where you want to be, take small steps and small rewards.

"Happiness does not come from doing easy work but from the afterglow of satisfaction that comes after the achievement of a difficult task that demanded our best."

Theodore Isaac Rubin

Recap: Reward yourself for choosing to make a difference.

***

If you have enjoyed Choose to Change: It's your life, then you'll love my next book in the series, Choose to Count: Start with you: 14 tweaks for self-esteem and confidence. Go and take a look on Amazon now.

Checklist and Journal Offer

Here is your checklist:

https://BookHip.com/FLHJZKF

I'd like to offer you a free PDF copy of a printable journal, presently selling on Amazon. It will help you to keep track of progress and give you clear guidelines to follow.

Get your free journal by following this link:

https://BookHip.com/XNNGFQ

The journal follows the same chapter headings as this book and will aid you in keeping things together. Once you have your journal, you'll be on my contact list and I'll keep you updated about new books and a few words of inspiration.

If you have trouble downloading your journal, drop me a line at:

jacquipennauthor@gmail.com

Other Books by Jacqui Penn

Choose to Count: Start with you - 14 tweaks for self-esteem and confidence (Book 2)

Choose to Create: Make the day yours – 6 early morning actions for taking control of your day (Book 3)

Choose to Commit: Make new habits stick - An easy and proven system for achieving lasting lifestyle changes (Book 4)

This Year I shall… A 52-week guided journal to make new habits stick (for Book 4)

A Year of Uplifting Inspiration: 365 days of positivity and Inspiration

Choose to Change Journal (for Book 1)

Links mentioned

Page   16
http://www.psykosyntese.dk/a-196/

Page   44
The life-changing magic of tidying:
A simple, effective way to banish
clutter forever by Marie Kondo

Page   54
www.youtube.com/watch?v=yfT8Ts6
wPFs

Page   82
www.mentalhealth.org.uk/a-to-
z/d/diet-and-mental-health

Page   84
www.healthy-holistic-living.com/2-
ways-water-improves-mental-
health.html

Acknowledgements

Thank you for reading Choose to Change. Your honest review on Amazon will help future readers decide if they want to take a chance on a new-to-them author.

My heartfelt thanks to Stephen Aldridge, Glinys Graham, Susette Butler, and Nola Cooper for their continuous help and support.

I also thank the people who read this, who didn't wish to be named, but gave me valuable feedback. You made a difference! You know who you are, thank you.

Most of all, I thank Tim, my sounding board, my inspiration and my friend.

About Jacqui

Jacqui Penn spends her time between Kent, England, and the Andalusian hillsides in Spain. When she's not writing, she can be found walking her dogs and mulling over ideas for her next book.

Through many ups and downs she has always managed to be a survivor, and believes a positive approach will conquer most of life's challenges.

www.jacquipenn.co.uk

www.facebook.com/jacquipennauthor

https://twitter.com/jacquipenn

www.pinterest.com/jacquipenn1

Printed in Great Britain
by Amazon

13757287R00078